HOOKED

— ON —

RIDDLES

HOOKED

— ON —

RIDDLES

A GUIDE TO TEACHING KIDS MATH, SCIENCE,
ENGLISH, AND OTHER SUBJECTS
USING FUN WORD PLAYS AND SILLY JOKES

MARY QUIJANO

Skyhorse Publishing

Except where noted, all names have been fictionalized to protect the individuals' privacy.

Skyhorse Publishing books may be purchased in bulk at special discounts for sales promotion, corporate gifts, fund-raising, or educational purposes. Special editions can also be created to specifications. For details, contact the Special Sales Department, Skyhorse Publishing, 307 West 36th Street, 11th Floor, New York, NY 10018 or info@skyhorsepublishing.com.

Skyhorse® and Skyhorse Publishing® are registered trademarks of Skyhorse Publishing, Inc.®, a Delaware corporation.

Visit our website at www.skyhorsepublishing.com.

10 9 8 7 6 5 4 3 2 1

Library of Congress Cataloging-in-Publication Data

Quijano, Mary.
  Hooked on riddles : a guide to teaching kids math, science, English, and other subjects using fun word plays and silly jokes / Mary Quijano.
    pages cm
  ISBN 978-1-61608-640-4 (pbk. : alk. paper)
1. Educational games. 2. Riddles, Juvenile. I. Title.
  LB1029.G3Q55 2012
  371.33'7--dc23
                        2012005902
ISBN: 978-1-61608-640-4

Printed in China

Contents

This book is dedicated to the memory of my sweet mother, Marjorie Nowel. She has always been my inspiration and biggest fan.

HOOKED

— ON —

RIDDLES

Introduction

Kids have an insatiable appetite for riddles. They love to giggle at the silly answers and to share riddles they've made up or have found in books. They find reason to celebrate when they figure out an answer or are able to share a riddle of their own!

For many years I've been injecting riddles into my daily curriculum and found that the more I employed these creative mind joggers, the more I enjoyed seeing the results—and the more the kids were engaged during class. I was pleased to see even the most reluctant students participate with effort and genuine interest during riddle time. The more I relied on a daily dose of riddles in the classroom, the more the riddles began to take on a life of their own. My students and I are now hooked!

Other teachers started asking me how I use riddles and wanted me to share some with them. I started providing the teachers in my grade level with random weekly riddles. Eventually, I became more precise at matching riddles to the current themes and topics we were studying in our curriculum. It's fun to share with my fellow teachers the joy I find in using riddles in my classroom.

Some years ago, my use of riddles in the classroom was featured in a newspaper column at the beginning of the school year. The energetic response I received from fellow teachers, parents, grandparents, and others who spend a great deal of time with children to that column encouraged me to write this book.

Even though this book shows how riddles are used in a classroom setting, the riddles and strategies inside can be used by anyone who works with children on a regular basis. Whether you are a day care provider, a babysitter, a nurse, a teacher, a doting grandparent, or a parent with little ones of your own, this book will start you on the way to a healthy dose of daily riddles. It's, in all actuality, a book for kids of all ages!

Enjoy your journey through the delightful world of riddles with Mrs. Q and her sharp thinking Riddlemasters. There's only one warning before you begin: Riddles are habit forming. If you consistently share them with the little ones in your life, you will begin to crave them as well, and they will eventually take on a life of their own. Are you willing to enjoy and share silly fun every day? Mrs. Q and her Riddlemasters challenge you to take the plunge!

You and your kids will soon be hooked!

Chapter 1

The Beginning of the Year
or Who's in Third?

The year begins in the usual way. I check to see that all the students on my roll have arrived and warmly greet the parents, gently convincing them that they may leave and that their children will be just fine. I meet the new students who have heard all sorts of stories about their new teacher. It's confusing, scary, challenging, and exciting. That is, the *kids* are fine! *I'm* the one who needs reassurance. You'd think that, for as many years as I've been teaching, the first day of school would become easier after time. Yet, I still have a hard time quelling my fears as I try to keep my blood pressure in check, and my sleep-deprived eyes open.

Finally, things calm down. The last nervous parent has gone; the third graders have greeted one another and are now seated at their desks. They're looking at me for some sort of direction. That's the perfect time for the first question of importance:

"Why do birds fly south for the winter?" works well.

Of course, in trying to impress their nervous teacher, the third graders come up with all sorts of explanations:

"They are looking for warmer weather."

"That's what they do every year when the leaves start to fall from the trees."

"It's called migration; the birds go in search of places where they can find good weather."

But nothing satisfies me. So I repeat, this time emphasizing the word "fly." The looks on their puzzled faces make me feel more comfortable. Finally they are as unsure as I am! Now we're getting somewhere!

"Think about the word *fly*," I instruct.

They can't figure it out, so I ask them if they would like to walk from Ohio to Texas. That's when someone begins to realize that the answer has nothing to do with migration at all. It's about flying instead of walking. Of course! The light bulb goes on and someone comes up with the idea that the birds fly south because it is too far to walk!

The ice is broken, the birds are flying, and the year has officially begun. We all feel better!

Here are some riddles about school and other topics that are near and dear to the hearts of those young ones in your life. These silly riddles are guaranteed to help them smile away any scholarly fears or nervous thoughts they might experience about that first day of school—no matter what grade they are entering.

Before you enjoy these school riddles, take a look at some important points to guide you in using riddles with sharp young minds:

- Working with riddles sharpens our thinking skills. To be successful, you need to stop and analyze clues that lead to the answer.
- Emphasize the important clues so that the young riddle-masters know which ideas or words will direct them to the answer.
- Avoid giving the answers to the riddles, even if it means letting one or two go unanswered. You can always come back to it later and try again!

RIDDLES: School Time

Why did the kid walk backwards to school?
It was back to school day.

What's the difference between a teacher and a train?

A train says "choo choo!"
A teacher says "Throw that gum away! Don't chew chew!"

What's the difference between a teacher and a doughnut?
You can't dunk a teacher in a glass of milk.

How can you tell if a school is haunted?
It has school spirit.

Why was the teacher cross-eyed?
She couldn't control her pupils!

What do you get when you cross a vampire and a teacher?
A blood test.

Imagine you are in a school with no doors, no windows, and no furniture. How would you get out?
Stop imagining!

What's a snake's favorite subject in school?
Hiss-tory.

What's the hardest part about taking a test?
The answers.

How did Patrick do on his bubble test?
He blew it.

Why did the student bring scissors into the cafeteria?
He wanted to cut in the lunch line.

What's worse than finding a worm in your apple?
Finding half a worm!

What happened to the bad egg in the lunchroom?
It got eggs-pelled.

Why did the boy put a dictionary in his pants?
Because he wanted to be a smarty pants.

What is white when dirty and black when clean?
A blackboard.

Why are unsharpened pencils not very smart?
They don't make a point.

Why did the student leave school with a chair?
His teacher told him to take a seat.

Why did Johnny eat his homework?
His teacher said it was a piece of cake.

Why did the teacher give smart Alec an A+?
He made a wisecrack.

Why does the invisible man have trouble in school?
The teacher always marks him absent.

What school does the alphabet go to?
L-M-N-tary.

What's in a song but not in a tune? What's in the sun, but not in
the moon? What's out of range but still in sight?
The letter "S."

How does an eye doctor say good-bye?
I L B C N U.

If you want to write a report about Antarctica, what should you write with?
A ballpoint penguin.

What's an eight-letter word that usually only has one letter in it?
Envelope.

What happens once in a minute, twice in a moment, but never in an hour?
The letter "M."

When is corn like a quiz?
When it's popped.

What's green and round and goes camping?
A boy sprout.

What did the cowboy say to the pencil?
"Draw!"

What kind of jokes did Einstein tell?
Wisecracks.

If you're a bee, how do you get to school?
You take the buzz.

What do you call a smart clock?
Clockwise.

How many months have twenty-eight days?
All of them!

Which day is the hottest day of the week?
Sunday.

What day of the week do chickens hate?
Fry-day.

Does February March?
No, but April May.

What month does the most walking?
March!

What made the computer squeak?
Somebody stepped on the mouse.

What did the computer say when it fell off the table?
"That megahertz!"

WHAT'S A WITCH'S FAVORITE SUBJECT?

SPELLING!

Chapter 2

Critical Thinking Skills *or* Treat with Care, It's a Jungle Out There

*C*ritical *Thinking Skills*. When we first began qualifying thinking skills as "critical," I couldn't help but think of news reports telling us that a situation was critical, or someone was in critical condition in the hospital. *How*, I wondered, *did thinking skills earn the rank of bordering on fatal or being beyond hope? How are we going to take those little ones through the halls of near fatality and hopelessness?*

Then I looked at the situation from the other side of the student desk.

"Oh no, she's looking at me and I wasn't listening. I have no idea what she asked, but the question mark on her face and the raised eyebrow pointing at me are signs of impending doom. This is life or death! I may not make it until lunch time!"

That situation can be rather critical for a little one whose main concern at any certain moment is whether he should get the salad or try to brave the steak fingers for lunch!

So how do we get children to look at life critically? How do we get these critical thinking skills of retelling, comprehending, analyzing, comparing, and transferring into their mental workouts?

As painlessly as possible.

Riddles come to the rescue again! Sometimes without warning, I'll ask a riddle question like the one mentioned on the first day of school (chapter 1). I let them try to answer it, and then I ask it again emphasizing the key word.

This is what it might sound like:

"Which is heavier, a ton of bricks or a ton of feathers?"

After someone tells me that the bricks are heavier I would repeat the question with special emphasis on the word "ton."

"Which is heavier, a *ton* of bricks or a *ton* of feathers?"

If that doesn't help, then I tell them that the key word is "ton," By then they have the idea that we aren't comparing bricks or feathers, we're comparing tons! And a ton is a ton, regardless of what you're weighing!

Another skill that helps in deciphering riddles is that of looking at something from a different perspective or point of view. We need to look at our situation or our questions from various vantage points and think of different meanings that could be imbedded in the question. For example, "Why did the chicken cross the road?" could have a plethora of answers. It all depends on factors such as the location or the condition of the chicken.

One day at recess, I offered the Riddlemasters extra recess if they could come up with an original riddle that had something to do with our surroundings. While they were thinking of a way to earn those precious extra minutes of recess, the silence was broken by the cars passing by. That gave one of the Riddlemasters an idea:

"Why did the car drive past the school?" she suggested.

A flurry of answers was immediately offered. "To go to the next grade . . . . To get past elementary and on to middle school . . . To go play hooky . . . To go do its homework . . . Because the light was green!"

As the answers died down, the anxious students all wanted to know what the correct answer was.

"I forget!" she confessed.

"That's fine, they're all good answers! That earns you all five extra minutes."

That was a rare time when there was a tangible reward for coming up with riddles. Riddle time is always a reward in itself. It's a great attention-getter and always greeted with smiles.

Some days I let the Riddlemasters choose a riddle from the riddle bag. The student reading the riddle has the responsibility of selecting the relevant clues that will lead to the answer. Giving the answer is strictly forbidden. As the Riddlemasters' skill levels develop, no one asks for the answer, but they beg for relevant clues.

Here are some animal riddles that can be solved by isolating key information or by looking at the question from a different point of view. Animal riddles are especially effective because children love and identify with animals. As you solve these, see if you can identify clues that help you solve the riddle. That's a tricky job for a child, and riddle solving could take on critical dimensions if the correct clues aren't identified and shared.

You may have to handle these riddles with intensive care. Remember, it's a jungle out there for those emerging thinkers!

But first, here are some critical points to remember.

- Help your riddlemasters by emphasizing or stressing the key word that will lead them to solve the question as in the *ton of bricks* riddle.

- Think of what the subject can or cannot do or what objective the subject has for his action and make that part of your answer. That's how the Riddlemasters arrived at such diverse answers for the *why did the car drive past the school* question. Each answer reflected a different reason a person might have for getting past school.

- Use riddles whenever you have a couple of free minutes. Remember, kids *love* riddles! What a magnificent tool you have to help them develop their thinking skills. You will find, as Mrs. Q did, that the day is filled with two-minute segments that *beg* to be filled by a quick fun thinking session full of riddles!

- Cut up riddles with their answers and put them in a Riddle Bag or box for those times when you have a couple of minutes and don't have a riddle handy. Your riddlemasters will all want an opportunity to choose a riddle from the bag, so have a fair system in place for choosing volunteers. Reinforce the fact that they may only help their fellow riddlemasters arrive at the answer by giving clues and choosing key words!

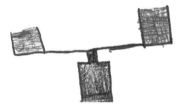

RIDDLES: Critical Thinking Animal Riddles

Can you pick out clues to help solve the riddle?

Why did the chicken cross the playground?
To get to the other slide!

Why did the fish cross the ocean?
To get to the other tide.

Why did the spider cross the road?
To get to her Web site.

Why did the turkey cross the road?
He wanted to prove he wasn't a chicken!

Why did the turtle cross the road?
To get to the shell station.

Why did the monster cross the road?
To eat the chicken.

Why did the rooster cross the road?
To prove he wasn't chicken!

Why couldn't the peanut butter cross the road?
Because there was a traffic jam.

How do snakes swim across a river?
They do the crawl.

What do you get when you cross an elephant with a mole?
Very big holes in your garden!

Why didn't the dinosaur cross the road? There weren't any roads back then!

How do snakes swim across a river?
They do the crawl.

What do you get when you cross an elephant with a mole?
Very big holes in your garden!

What do you get when you cross a chicken with a cat?
A scaredy-cat.

What do you get when you cross a chicken with a cat?

A scaredy-cat.

What do you get when you cross a computer with an elephant?

A five-ton know-it-all.

What do you get when you cross a cat with a canary?

A peeping tom.

What do you call a cow that eats grass?

A lawn moo-er.

What is a puppy on a mountain peak?

Top dog.

What do you call a puppy on a mountain peak?   **Top dog**

Why couldn't the Dalmatian hide from his mom?
Because he was already spotted!

What do you get if you cross a centipede and a parrot?
A walkie-talkie.

What do you call a girl with a frog on her head?
Lily.

What do you get when you cross a bumblebee with a rabbit?
A honey bunny.

What do rabbits put in their computers?
Hoppy disks.

What do you get when you cross a sheep with a porcupine?
An animal that can knit its own sweaters!

What's gray and has a trunk?
A mouse on vacation!

What do you get when you cross a sheep with a porcupine?
An animal that can knit its own sweaters!

What do you call a goat that tells jokes?
A silly goat.

What do you put on a pig's feet when they are dry?
Oinkment!

What do you get when a horse and a sheep move in next door?
New neigh-baas.

What do you get if you cross a saber-toothed tiger and a flower?
I don't know, but I wouldn't try to smell it.

What do you get when you cross a kangaroo and a raccoon?
A fur coat with pockets.

What game do mice like best?
Hide and squeak.

What's a penguin's favorite game?
Freeze tag.

What's a grasshopper's favorite sport?
Cricket.

Why were night baseball games invented?
Because bats like to sleep in the daytime.

What animal is best at hitting a baseball?
A bat.

What's a shark's favorite game?   Swallow the leader!

Help!

What sport do owls play?
Hootball.

What game do cows like to play at parties?
Moosical chairs.

Why did the baseball player get scared?
He saw a bat.

Why don't cobras like baseball?
They only get three strikes.

In dog baseball, where does the manager sit?
In the dogout!

What do you call a player who falls asleep in the bullpen?
A bulldozer.

What is the best way to catch a fish?
Have someone throw it to you!

Who does a canine quarterback throw to?
A Labrador receiver.

What kind of cat likes to go bowling?
An alley cat.

How do elephants talk to each other?
On the elephone!

What did the worm say when he was taking a shower?

"Ah, I like it wormer."

What kinds of horses go out after dark?

Nightmares!

Which pets like to lie around the house?

Carpets.

What did the bunny say about the story?

"It needs a hoppy ending."

What animal talks the most?

A yak!

How many skunks live in our neighborhood?
Quite a phew!

Why is a skunk rich?
Because it has a lot of scents.

Why couldn't the skunk use the phone?
It was out of odor!

How does a sick kangaroo get better?
It has a hoperation!

What does a shark get when he loses a tooth?
A sand dollar!

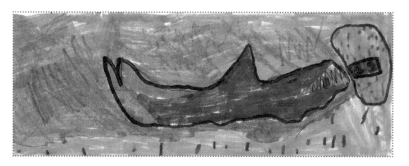

Where do bees go after they get married?
On a honeymoon!

Why shouldn't you tell a secret to a pig?
Because he's a squealer!

What do you call a fly without wings?
A walk!

HOOKED ON **RIDDLES**

Chapter 3

Metamorphically Speaking *or* Riddles Rock!

So, you've been wondering what's the difference between a solid and a liquid, between a sedimentary and a metamorphic rock, why caves don't cave in, what causes a volcano to erupt, why the sky is blue and money is green, why dust never seems to go away, and why cobwebs fill your head on a Monday morning.

What is the meaning of life? Actually, most elementary school students could care less, but they do wonder why it's important to know that the openings of caves are sometimes called sinkholes or they want a clue to help them remember that it's the deciduous trees whose leaves change color and fall each year.

Riddles become valuable word plays to help children (and adults, too) remember terminology. Such is the case with deciduous trees. As we were playing our vocabulary games in the classroom, I took apart the word "deciduous" and pulled out "decide." Then I let the Riddlemasters play with that for a while. That's how we ended up remembering the term. Deciduous trees can't decide what color they want their leaves to be, so they change their color in the fall, lose them, and start all over in the spring.

To introduce a science chapter on caves I declared that I had a sinking feeling that morning. I continued by telling the students we were beginning a new unit in science. On the first page of the reading material the students saw a picture of caves. The light started to flicker in their riddlemaster eyes.

We read that many caves are discovered by venturing through a sinkhole. Then the spelunker lights were ignited on the cave hats. We were on a roll! There was no stopping us!

How do we remember the difference between stalagmites and stalactites? That one's easy, as the stalagmites are on the ground, thus the "g" in the word, and they just "mite" reach the ceiling if they grow enough. Of course, the stalactites earned their name because they hang onto the ceiling, thus the "c" in their word, and they must hold on "tite" or they'll fall! And everyone knows the grouchy stalagmite told the stalactite to quit dripping on him! However, if they ever do connect, they become a column, which could lead to some interesting reading. We're rocking now!

These rock solid gems were interjected into the material as we continued our study of caves. The result was twofold. The material was much more engaging and it was easier for the kids to remember.

The reward for all this study was a field trip to nearby limestone caverns. Our tour guide stopped us at the entrance to the caves and explained how the caverns had been discovered, telling us that we were about to enter the sinkhole that opened this cave network. At the word "sinkhole" the kids all turned around and looked at me with anticipation. They didn't say a word but their eyes were begging me to use my sinking feeling comment. When our guide asked if there were any questions before we descended into the caves, one of the Riddlemasters in the back asked what the grouchy stalagmite said to the stalactite. The guide didn't hear it, but we all grinned because we knew the answer.

Another example of employing riddles to help learning came in our study of volcanoes. There was some off-task behavior and chattering in the room that needed redirecting.

"Don't erupt while I'm talking," was all I needed to declare.

"But we're having such a blast!" was the reply.

(Luckily, the Riddlemasters know that Mrs. Q lavas them very much.)

At any rate, do you want your little ones to know that you lava them? Are you all searching for answers to the science questions around you? The following riddles will do the trick. Metamorphically speaking, these riddles rock!

Here are more rock solid ideas to guide you in using riddles.

- Riddles help children remember information and terms in a fun way.
- Break up parts of long words, connect those parts to easier words, and you have created a tool for identifying that word. That's what Mrs. Q and the Riddlemasters did with the word "deciduous."
- Find words that sound similar to terms you need to remember. Make a connection, like the "sedimental" dinosaur and the fossil you'll find in the first science riddle.

- You will find that as you use riddles and word plays, it will become easier to develop your own clever replies, as Mrs. Q and the Riddlemasters did with the volcano lesson. You will be bursting with clever statements that you never thought possible.
- Riddles will unite you and your riddlemasters just like they did at the field trip in the above example. The more you speak the language of riddles, the more you and your riddlemasters will understand each other and appreciate each other's questions and creative answers.

RIDDLES: Science Riddles That Rock

Why did the dinosaur cry when it saw a fossil?
It got sedimental.

What kind of music do cave dwellers like?
Rock!

What did the metamorphic rock say to the sedimentary rock?
"You wouldn't believe the pressure I've been under!"

How many miles of unexplored caves are there?
If they're unexplored, you don't know.

What did the grouchy stalagmite say to the stalactite?

"Quit dripping on me!"

Why did the cave talk so much?

It had a big mouth.

How did the hole know a cave was near?

It had a sinking feeling.

What kind of bats do you find at a circus?

Acro-bats!

Why was the cave scared of the underground stream?

The stream is always springing up on it.

Why did the explorer stop visiting caves?

He got tired of the hole business.

What did one mountain say to the other mountain after the earthquake?

"It wasn't my fault."

Where are the biggest diamonds in America?

In a baseball park.

What did one erupting volcano say to the other erupting volcano?

"Go with the flow!"

Why was the deciduous tree always changing colors?
He couldn't decide what color he wanted to be.

What is a tree's favorite drink?
Root beer.

How did the flower ride the bike?
With its petals.

What did one dandelion say to the other dandelion?
"Take me to your weeder."

What do you call a mountain that looks when it's not supposed to?
A peek.

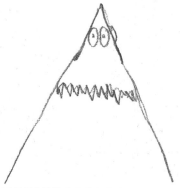

Where's the best place to find books about trees?
In a branch library.

When do asteroids like water?
When there are meteor showers.

What does a movie theater marquee cause when it falls into the ocean?
A title wave.

did the river say to the sea?
"It was nice running into you."

What happens if you throw a green brick into the Red Sea?
It gets wet!

How do you begin a story about coconuts?

"Once a palm a tree…"

What did the pumpkin say when the farmer asked how he was?

"I'm vine, thank you."

Why was the dog jealous of the tree?

The tree had a better bark.

Why was the tree afraid of the dog?

The dog stole its bark.

Why didn't the tree move when the dog barked at it?

He was barking up the wrong tree.

Why didn't the tree move when the dog barked at it?
He was barking up the wrong tree.

Why should you be careful if it's raining cats and dogs?
You might step in a poodle.

What did the dirt say to the rain?
"Stop pouring or my name will be mud."

What do bats like to do on the weekend?
Just hang around.

Six men were under a small umbrella. Why didn't any of them get wet?
It wasn't raining.

When is the best time to visit the library?
When there's a title wave!

What goes up when the rain comes down?
An umbrella.

What's a good book to read during a hurricane?
Gone with the Wind.

What do you get when the sun goes surfing?
A heat wave.

What did the wind say to the screen door?

"Just passing through!"

What did summer say to spring?

"Help, I'm going to fall!"

Why did the dog stay in the shade?

It didn't want to be a hotdog.

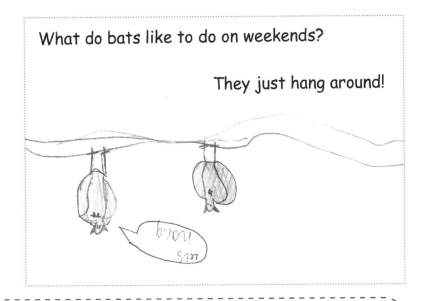

What side of the body has the most bones?

The inside.

What did one eye say to the other eye?

"Between you and me, there is something that smells!"

What do you call a penguin in the desert?

Lost.

What kind of sharks makes good carpenters?

Hammerheads.

What did the boy octopus say to the girl octopus?
"I want to hold your hand, hand, hand, hand, hand, hand, hand, hand."

What's the difference between a fly and a mosquito?
A mosquito can fly, but a fly can't mosquito!

What did the baby volcano say to the mommy volcano?

I lava you.

Chapter 4

It All Adds Up *or* The Ultimate Word Problem

D o you sometimes have numbers swimming in your head and you just can't make heads or tails of them? Are feet, meters, grams, liters, quarts, and pounds all weighing heavily on your mind? Sometimes my third graders and I feel the same. Numbers and units of measure can be downright confusing. Which unit of measure is the best to use? When do you add or subtract? Are there any key words that might give you a hint?

In today's world of higher order thinking skills, the strategy has taken on more importance than the actual computation. Many word problems on math tests don't even require a completed answer anymore. Rather, deciding on a method of solving the problem and choosing the correct numbers to work with are the challenges at hand.

Gone are the days when a third grader's biggest worry is how to "borrow" or "carry" when adding or subtracting in working math problems. Those are necessary skills, but in order to get to that step, third graders need more sophisticated skills. In attacking and solving a word problem, they need to locate the necessary and pertinent data and disregard information put there to distract them. It is imperative that they identify words and numbers that are needed to plan the solution. They need to keep track of and deal with important information while they work through it, step by step.

The process of finding the answer to a riddle requires the same thinking skills. You could think of a riddle as the ultimate word problem!

One day I had the opportunity to use some of those necessary problem solving and riddle solving skills. It was my turn to learn first-hand how important it is to keep track of important numbers and how successfully a major distraction could work to my advantage.

Early one evening I was at the grocery store when I ran into one of my students. Actually, I almost ran him over with my shopping cart because he stopped dead in his tracks with a look of total disbelief on his face.

"Mrs. Q, what are you doing here?" he gasped.

I assured him that I was hungry and needed some food, but I promised to return to school promptly. Whew! I could see the look of relief on his face as I imagined him reassuring himself that

I would indeed head back to my cot at school, thus guaranteeing my presence there the following morning.

Later at the checkout counter I was faced with a dilemma. I only had a $20 bill in my pocket. No credit cards or checkbook to rely on. As the goods were sliding along the conveyor belt to the cash register, I began to worry that I wouldn't have enough money for everything I had found. The line of people behind me looked hostile, and it could get ugly and downright dangerous if the total passed the twenty-dollar mark.

I chuckled as I remembered telling my students how I round the cost of each item and then estimate the total cost before I get to the checkout counter. But at this moment, it was too late to practice what I preached.

It was time for Plan Q!

That's when I turned to the person behind me eying the amount of merchandise and the $20 bill in my hand. I bravely attempted to diffuse the mounting tension with a question of numeric importance.

"Do you know why a quarter is smarter than a nickel?"

Total confusion, successful distraction, and the tension was dispelled for a moment.

"Huh?" was the reply.

The moment of truth. The grand total: $20.17! Horrors! What will I do?

"Wait! Let me repeat! Why is a quarter smarter than a nickel?" I tried again.

"I don't know," came an impatient reply from behind me, "but here's a quarter!"

"That's close! Because it had more cents! And now so do I. Thanks!" I celebrated.

Saved by the question! I let my new grocery store friend keep the change from the quarter and smiled as I thought of my Riddle-masters and how I couldn't wait to tell them how successfully I had transferred the use of riddles into the real world of grocery stores!

Here are some math riddles that might save you in a tight spot, or when the numbers just don't add up. These also have key words that will direct you to the solution of the question posed. Some have information to distract you from finding the solution so proceed with caution!

Here are more important points to guide you in using riddles with those sharp young minds:

- As you work with riddles, you will become more successful at deciding which information is there to confuse or distract you.
- Riddles effectively use those higher order-thinking skills that are so important in problem solving. The process of identifying the pertinent information and disregarding the distracting data, and then deciding what to do with the necessary information, is exactly what a riddlemaster has to do in solving word problems.

- As you direct your riddlemasters to the correct information, make them aware of the process they are using to eliminate distractors and analyze useful data. At first you will need to tell them which information is necessary and which they need to disregard. But they will soon become proficient at this process.
- Even Mrs. Q has learned to manipulate the distracting information factor to her advantage. Did you notice how she used all that math information to justify sharing her silly grocery store story?

RIDDLES: **Math Time Riddles**

Look for the key words that help you decide how to answer them!

When is math a heavy subject?
When you have to carry the numbers.

What did one workbook say to the other?
"I have a lot of problems."

What has three feet, no toes, and can't walk?
A yardstick.

What has four legs and no head?
A table.

What goes up and never comes down?
Your age.

What grows smaller as time goes by?
A candle.

Who can jump higher than a ten-story building?
Anyone. Buildings can't jump!

What's Roman and grows on walls?
IV

There were ten cats on a boat. One jumped off. How many were left?

None. They were copycats!

How did the magician cut the sea in half?

With a sea saw!

Where do you weigh a whale?

At the whaleweigh station!

Why do fish have scales?

So they can be weighed.

If a butcher's shirt size is XXL and his shoe size is 12, what does he weigh?

Meat. He's a butcher!

What did one parallel line say to the other?

"Why don't we ever meet?"

What do you call an octopus that's gone away?
An octagon!

Why did the boy put numbers on himself?
So his friends could count on him.

If twelve inches equal one foot, what is above a foot?
An ankle.

Why did the riddlemaster take a ruler to bed with her?
So she could find out how long she slept.

Why is our hand less than twelve inches long?
Any longer and it would be a foot.

Why did the boy's mother knit him three socks for his birthday?
Because he grew another foot.

How many sides does a mouse have?
Two—inside and outside!

What side of a turkey has the most feathers?
The outside.

Is a hammer a useful tool in math class?
No, you need multipliers!

What's the fastest way to double your money?
Fold it in half!

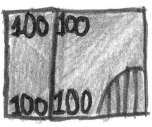

Why didn't the dime jump off the hill after the nickel?
The dime had more cents!

If there are twelve 25-cent candies in a dozen, how many
50-cent candies are in a dozen?
Twelve, of course!

What did the girl say when she learned how to count money?
"It all makes cents to me now!"

The duck went into a grocery store to buy some popcorn but didn't have any money. What did he do?

He put it on his bill.

What can fly without wings?

Time.

How many hours until a fish goes to work?

Tuna half.

What kind of tree comes in twos?

A pear tree.

HOOKED ON RIDDLES

Q: What time is it?
A: I'm not sure, but it's not five yet.
Q: How do you know?
A: Because my mom said to be home by five and I'm not home yet.

What do you call a dog that tells time?
A watchdog.

If you invite a clock for dinner, what will it ask for?
Seconds.

What time of year do you jump on a trampoline?
Spring time!

What do you call two doctors?
Pair-a-medics.

How much dirt is in a hole one-foot wide, one-foot long, and one-foot deep?
None. There's no dirt in a hole!

Mrs. Q: If you had 50 cents in your pocket and you asked your dad for another 50 cents, how much would you have?

Riddlemaster: 50 cents.

Mrs. Q: You obviously don't know how to add.

Riddlemaster: You obviously don't know my dad!

What is a duck's favorite math problem?

Quacktions!

Chapter 5

Monster Mas *or* This Is Only a Test

"Monster Mas" is not a typographical error or misspelling. "Mas" means "more" in Spanish. One of our riddle suppliers started using the word in the subject line of his emails because he knew we had a Spanglish element in our class. He'd write, "Mas riddles for the riddlemasters," meaning of course, "More riddles for the riddlemasters."

He seemed fairly proud of this and we think it might be the only Spanish word he knows. So the third graders congratulated him, hoping to boost his self-esteem. They know that grown-ups can be awfully fragile.

Anyway, he sent us "mas" so often that eventually he simply referred to the riddles themselves as "mas," as in "I'll send more mas for the riddlemasters next week."

After a while the students and I began referring to his riddles as mas and began to refer to our new riddle friend as Mr. Riddle. We all believe he lives up north somewhere, where the birds start flying south in the winter.

Inevitably, Mr. Riddle started sending us an end of the week email called the *Friday monster mas,* which is of course a play on the title of "The Monster Mash," a 1962 recording by Bobby "Boris" Pickett that gets revived on the radio every Halloween.

The Friday monster mas always had riddles featuring monsters, ghosts, witches, vampires, and other scary creatures. Mr. Riddle figured that monster jokes were perennial favorites among kids. They're a way of dealing with fears and mastering the unknown. They're a way of defusing the fears of childhood. And let's face it, they're silly fun.

He sent them on Fridays because it seemed like a fun way to end the week and start the weekend. We also believe he chose that day because Friday is the day when TV and theaters like to schedule monster movies.

That worked for me. But I had another use for the Friday monster mas. I turned it into a double feature.

Third graders in the state of Texas must take their first state mandated math and reading tests in the spring. The math test can be downright scary and unnerving. These nervous third graders needed reassurance that they had the skills and tools needed to excel on both tests.

So we devoted some class time on Friday mornings to skills directly related to the material and format of the upcoming tests. If the Riddlemasters remained focused, then their reward was a session of monster mas supplied by their favorite correspondent, Mr. Riddle. It gave them something to look forward to, and reminded them that we can face our fears and overcome them by using our thinking skills. Besides, the batch of silly monster mas was always a lot of fun!

I reminded my Riddlemasters that test questions are a lot like riddles. You need to read them carefully, think about what they are asking, identify important information, disregard irrelevant information, and be able to prove your answers. That way you can approach a challenging testing session as you do a challenging riddle: confidently, with a minimal amount of fear. The goal is to come out successful and smiling.

One Friday morning after a draining session of working through tricky test questions and problems, we had a monster riddle that needed analyzing. In guiding them to the answer, I modeled the same process that we used in working through some of those scary math problems. It went like this:

"What do you get when you cross a cucumber with a werewolf?" I asked. The students looked confused.

"I'll help you. We can take it one step at a time and develop the answer together. What does a processed cucumber become?" I directed.

"A pickle?" came a doubtful answer from the back of the room.

"Correct! Now what does a werewolf become?"

"Scary and hairy!" came the answer from the other side of the room.

"Excellent! We're almost there. Now, what does it take for a werewolf to become hairy?"

"A full moon," came the reply from another side of the room.

"Great. Now put all those answers together. Let me ask you again. What do you get when you cross a cucumber with a werewolf?" I repeated.

"A pickle that gets hairy when there's a full moon!" roared a group of students in the front of the room.

Gales of mirth accompanied the conquest of that riddle.

We had merrily discovered the answer by analyzing the information and taking it apart, piece by piece. It was then that I pointed out to my victorious Riddlemasters that the process is the same when working on math problems. Victory was as tasty as a pickle!

And so begin many Fridays in the class of the Riddlemasters. I direct them through a challenging session of higher order thinking skills needed to attack these somewhat scary tests. Their reward is a fun session of monster riddles, or monster mas.

Therefore, next time you have a troubled little one who is overcoming some fear, or who needs to think through something step by step, or who just wants to have some plain goofy fun, here is a monster-load of mas, uh, riddles! You'll have those little ones crying "mas, mas, mas!"

Here are some important points to remember in using riddles.

- Many times, answering a riddle involves taking apart the information. Look at each part of the riddle. Is there another way to refer to each part? After you've looked at each part and found other names for each one or determined how you can look at that part differently, put it all together again using the answers to each section. That's what the Riddlemasters did with the hairy pickle riddle.

- Remind your young ones that they, too, have the skills to overcome new and unfamiliar situations and challenges. At first, riddles are unknown, confusing territories. The more you work with them, the more proficient your young ones become in answering them.

- Use fun riddle sessions as rewards. You'll be surprised at the interest and excitement riddles generate. Motivate your young ones to complete a task with the promise of a riddle session after they've finished.

- Share your love of riddles with others. Let your friends know that you'd be thrilled if they would share some riddles with you! There just may be a riddle fanatic who would enjoy sharing with you. Making the riddle supplier a mystery adds to the delight of the riddles.

- To this day, this is all that any riddlemaster knows about the supplier of riddles in Mrs. Q's room. Mr. Riddle's first name is Mister. He lives up north in Riddle Command somewhere. His riddles come through email. Mr. Riddle rules when it comes to supplying riddles!

RIDDLES: Monster Mas!

Caution, super scary material ahead!

Why does Dracula watch the World Series?
He likes the bats!

What did the vampire say at bedtime?
"It's time to turn off the bite light."

How was the werewolf's party?
A howling success.

Why did the vampire dump her boyfriend?
Because he was a pain in the neck!

Who did the vampire marry?
The girl necks door.

Why did the vampire go to the orthodontist?
To improve his bite.

How did the vampire cross the ocean?
In a blood vessel.

Why did the vampire go to the drugstore?
He wanted something for his coffin!

Why did the vampire buy mouthwash at the drugstore?
He had bat breath!

Why did the little vampires stay up until midnight?
They were studying for a blood test.

What did the vampire catch after staying out all night?
A bat cold.

What did the vampire get from the snowman?
Frostbite.

What kind of jokes do vampires tell?
Neck-neck jokes.

What do you get when King Kong sneezes?
Out of the way.

How do you fix a broken jack-o-lantern?
With a pumpkin patch.

How do you stop a werewolf from howling in the back of a car?
Put him in the front.

What do you get when ghosts sneeze?
Booogers.

What kind of dog did Dracula want?
A bloodhound.

Dracula fell in love with a witch.
For him it was love at first bite.
For her it was love at first fright.

What do you call a witch doctor's mistake?
A voodoo boo-boo.

What magazine do witches read?
Good Housecreeping.

What do you call a witch in the desert?
A sandwitch.

What did the girl say to the ghost?
"Get a life!"

What do little ghosts wear when it rains?
Booo-ts and ghoulashes.

What did the mother ghost say to the baby ghost?

"Spook when you're spoken to."

How do ghosts cross the street?

Very scarefully.

What room did the ghost not dare to go into?

The living room.

What did the ghost's mother tell her child in the car?

"Put on your sheet belt."

HOOKED ON **RIDDLES**

Where do ghosts go to retire?

A ghost town.

What is a ghost's favorite ride at the amusement park?

The scary-go-round.

Where is the best place to build a haunted house?

On a dead end street.

What is big and hairy and flies 1,200 miles an hour?
King Kongcorde.

How did the skeleton know it was going to rain?
He could feel it in his bones.

Why didn't the skeleton go to the party?
Because he had no body to go with.

What do you call a skeleton that won't get out of bed?
Lazy bones.

HOOKED ON **RIDDLES**

What do monsters eat for breakfast?
Scream of wheat.

What's long and green and dangerous?
A herd of charging celery.

What did one jack-o-lantern say to the other jack-o-lantern?
"Cut it out!"

What do monsters wear when they're out in the sun?
Sun scream.

Why do mummies have trouble keeping friends?
They're too wrapped up in themselves.

Chapter 6

Write It Right *or* Playing with Words

W hich witch is which?

Homophones. They're a spelling nightmare! They sound the same, yet they're spelled and used differently. In the classroom we develop word clues to remember the more infamous of the homophones like to, too, and two. Then we spend some time making posters to help us remember the clues.

Riddles can help form mental posters that help us play with and remember those troublesome homophones. Hopefully in manipulating tricky homophones in riddles we will be better equipped to spell them on paper.

A homophone isn't the only puzzle a riddlemaster has to wrestle with. Working with words that have multiple meanings and determining the intended definition can be downright threatening to a young thinker.

Elementary school children, when faced with the task of determining which meaning of a word is being used in a given sentence, have difficulty choosing between similar meanings. The context of the word must be determined. It can be tricky and frustrating!

Aha! That's when riddles come in very handy. An extremely popular type of riddle is the one that uses a word out of context as an answer. The word belongs because of its other meanings. I like to ask the many meanings of a word when helping students arrive at the riddle's correct answer. When you do that with the little ones, you've just become their best friend by turning the tricky and frustrating into challenging and fun!

One day, the Riddlemasters were locating and identifying homophones that are commonly used in their reading. I used that opportunity to play with some riddles. After I reminded the class that a homophone is part of the answer, I asked them what happened to the young colt when she yelled a lot.

"A colt is a young horse. Use the homophone for horse in your answer."

Billy's hand shot up. "I know! He became a little hoarse!"

"Very good. Here's another. What makes a rabbit grumpy? Think of another word for rabbit. That's the homophone we're looking for."

"How about hare?" tried Emily.

"That's it! Now use that word's homophone to describe a bad day," I encouraged them.

"I got it!" shouted Joey. "A bad hair day makes it grumpy!"

We were hopping right along and had a couple of minutes while we got washed up before lunch so I asked them the golden question: "Does anyone have a riddle to share?"

"What did the rabbit give his girlfriend for Valentine's Day?" asked Scott.

"A hare hug?" chuckled Jeannie.

"Pretty funny, but not quite. It has something to do with what rabbits like to eat."

"They eat carrots!" said Chris.

Cindy had a knowledgeable grin on her face. "A ring. A one-carrot ring!" she answered with a smile.

The Riddlemasters energetically continued to share riddles. Scott's hand shot up again and I reminded them that everyone deserved a chance to share.

"Hey, I have a bear riddle!" added Allison authoritatively. "Why did the grizzly bear stay late at the party?"

"Because he was a beary party animal?" tried one of the riddlemasters.

"No. Let me help you. The word bear is in the answer," Allison declared.

"How about, he couldn't bear to leave," said Cathy with a grin.

"That's right!" proclaimed Allison. "Good job, Cathy!"

I interrupted the Riddlemasters to explain that the word "bear" wasn't used as a homophone in that example. It was used with a different meaning. It had one meaning in the question and a different one in the answer.

Scott's hand was waving energetically again, but I reminded him that he had already shared a riddle.

"But, Mrs. Q . . . .."

"It's ok, Scott. Let's give someone else a turn."

"Here's another. Why is it smart to go to a baseball game in the summer?" asked Pedro.

"Because you don't have to get up early to go to school the next day," lamented Marty.

"Not quite. Think about the heat in the summer. What do you call the people watching the game?" Pedro helped.

"It's hot and they're called fans," suggested Tommy.

"Wait, I got it!" proclaimed Louis. "Because there are lots of fans at a game!"

"And lots of hot dogs. Boy am I hungry," sighed Scott.

That's when I looked at the clock on the wall. "Oh my goodness! We should have been in the cafeteria for lunch ten minutes ago! Let's get moving!"

"That's what I've been trying to tell you," sighed Scott.

So whether you're reading or writing, deciding which spelling is correct or which meaning you want to employ, these riddles will help take some of the frustration out of the task at hand. But try not to miss lunch. Cafeteria food or not, you still have to eat!

Enjoy the following delicious riddles. The key is in the spelling of the homophone or the use of an alternate meaning.

Here are some points to remember before getting to the riddles.

- Homophones make excellent answers for riddles. Sometimes it's necessary to find a synonym first. In the bad hair day we started with a rabbit, used its synonym hare, and then changed to the homophone hair for the answer. Of course, kids don't need to know that you are employing all these skills, unless you want them to know how impressively clever they are.

HOOKED ON **RIDDLES**

- Words with multiple meanings also work well with riddles. When using words with multiple meanings, ask kids which meaning is being employed in the question and if that same meaning applies to the answer, as in the bear that couldn't bear to leave.
- If the answer is correct because of alternate meanings, such as fans at the baseball game, ask your riddlemasters to identify the two meanings that are being interchanged.
- If your youngsters try to interrupt, sometimes it's good to see why they are so insistent in sharing something. Those poor riddlemasters almost missed lunch one day!

What do two oceans do when they come together?

WaVe to each other

RIDDLES: Write it Right Using Homophones, Synonyms, and Words with Alternate Meanings

How do you tell if a bucket is not well?
It's a little pale.

Why do dragons sleep during the day?
So they can fight knights.

Why shouldn't you give someone a gate?
Because they might take a fence.

Why shouldn't you play cards in the jungle?
Too many cheetahs.

Why are there so many sails on boats?
So people will buy them.

What do you call a piece of wood with nothing to do?
Bored.

What happens when the frog's car breaks down?
It gets toad.

What kind of shoes do bears wear in the forest?
None. They have bare feet.

What's the difference between a tiger and a lion?
A tiger has the mane part missing.

What should you do if you hurt your toe?
Call a toe truck.

Did you hear about the man who doesn't have a left side?
He's all right now.

What do you call a rabbit's fur?
Hare hair.

How does a dog stop a VCR?

He presses the paws button.

What did the impatient stag say to his daughter?

"Hurry up, deer!"

Why did the bald man paint rabbits on his head?

Because from a distance, they looked like hares.

A man was driving to Austin. He saw a sign that said "Austin left."

So he turned around and went home.

Where do sneakers dance?

At the football.

HOOKED on **RIDDLES**

Why did the policeman stay in bed?
Because he was an undercover cop.

Which planet has the most jewelry?
Saturn. It has rings.

Where is the nearest place you can see stars?
On the U.S. flag.

Why did the farmer name his pig "Ink"?
Because it always ran out of the pen.

What did one car say to the other car when it was raining?
"I'm glad I have my hood on."

What did the beach say when the tide came in?
"Long time no sea!"

What did the whale say to the water?

Nothing. He just waved.

Why is it a bad idea to tell secrets on a farm?

Because the corn has ears.

What has keys but no door?

A piano.

Why did the robber take a bath?

So he could make a clean getaway.

Where did the sailors play cards?
On the deck.

How do turtles pay for things?
They shell out cash.

Why didn't the car feel well?
It had gas.

Why was Cinderella no good at soccer?
Because she kept running away from the ball.

What did Cinderella say when they took her picture?

"I hope my prints will come."

Why did the policeman arrest the cat?

Because of the kitty litter.

When is a car not a car?

When it turns into a parking lot.

What did the stamp say to the letter?

"Stick with me, and we'll go places!"

What runs all over town but never comes in?

The road.

What do you call a guy sleeping in front of the door?

Matt.

What do bikes do when they get old?

Retire.

What did the doctor say to the quiet lady in his office?

"You're a patient patient."

Why did the girl tiptoe past the medicine cabinet?

She didn't want to wake the sleeping pills.

Why did the woman put glue all over her head?

She had a splitting headache.

What's a personal foul?

Your own chicken.

Why are deer so poor ?

Because there's only one buck in the family.

Chapter 7

Blackboards and Ditto Sheets *or* Dinosaurs in Our Filing Cabinets

You will find that a daily dose of riddles creates a need for more riddles! Another side effect of this delightful medicine is the ability to develop your own answers that are totally justifiable! Actually, your riddlemasters will begin to develop answers that are more appropriate and many times cleverer than the prescribed ones.

You should now appreciate the fact that it's best not to give an answer to any riddle. If the clues aren't sufficient to figure out the answer, it's usually best left unanswered. Sometimes my class and I would revisit a tough riddle, and sometimes it went unanswered. If the riddlemasters can't determine the answer after numerous clues, then it probably isn't one they will understand or remember anyway.

Many times, however, this inability to come up with an answer is an opportunity to teach new vocabulary or to explain or describe something that the children have never experienced.

One day I asked the Riddlemasters the following question: "What gets blacker the more you clean it?" As a clue I told them it had something to do with the white board in front of the room.

"Hmmm . . . markers maybe?" someone ventured.

That's when I realized that these students had never gone to a school that had black or green chalkboards and they had never experienced the thrill of scraping their fingernails across a blackboard! So I found some school stories with blackboards and I described what they were like. I described the goose bumps reaction to the sound of fingernails scraping across the board and the itchy nose and watery eyes that resulted from chalk dust being dispersed into the air. After seeing some pictures in storybooks, the Riddlemasters understood the answer and realized that Mrs. Q was truly ancient to have spent most of her teaching years working with blackboards!

Another testimony to my timelessness as a teacher is my familiarity with ditto sheets and ditto masters. One day as I was cleaning out my files I found a ditto master with some accompanying purple copies. Ironically, the picture was in my "dinosaur" file and there was a cute little dinosaur on the paper. I ran to the classroom of a fellow teacher and exclaimed, "Look what I found!"

She responded with a questioning look. This young teacher said she had never seen a ditto sheet. I chose to believe that she simply didn't remember them.

If you're nodding your head now and saying, "Ditto masters, I remember them," then you are showing your age and probably hiding the gray as I do. Those were the days. I still remember getting a whiff of that ditto master fluid. It seems teachers smiled more back then.

I'm glad to say that riddles, unlike blackboards and ditto masters, are timeless. They reflect the times and sometimes help us identify with times gone by, while always causing us to smile. It's been proven that laughter is good therapy and helps keep you healthy. Riddles make you think and analyze and laugh all at the same time. What a prescription for happy intelligent children, then, to be sure they get a daily dose of riddles!

As your little ones get hooked on riddles, they will become very clever at contriving their own answers. In our classroom any answer that can be justified with a logical reason is acceptable. I am usually very pleased with the answers and reasons the kids come up with. I would like to share some of those golden responses. I'm sure that you will agree with me that some of the students' answers are more creative than the standard ones!

Here are some timeless recommendations for your use of riddles.

- True riddlemasters don't like you to tell them the answer. They do, however, crave clues that help them find the answer.
- There can be more than one correct answer to a riddle. When your young riddlemaster suggests an alternate answer, always ask him or her why such an answer was given. The reasoning will probably delight you!
- Enjoy the creative, original answers and applaud your riddlemasters for clever replies. Hearing how witty they are motivates them to continue using those thinking skills that helped them arrive at those answers and that delighted you

so much. Kids, just like adults, love to hear how clever and smart they are.

- Many times, you will find that riddles are excellent opportunities to discover what your young riddlemasters don't know or haven't experienced yet. If the clues you give them aren't sufficient, look at the answer, such as with the blackboard, and see if there is some topic or concept your young one hasn't explored yet.

- You might think about investing in a good pair of sunglasses. Your riddlemasters' answers are going to bedazzle you the more you work with riddles.

RIDDLES: Golden Responses

These have riddlemaster answers different from the standard answers.

Why did the man run around his bed at nighttime?
To catch up on his sleep.

Riddlemaster answer:
To catch his wife.

What did one volcano say to the other volcano?
Don't erupt while I'm talking.

Riddlemaster answers:
Are you having a blast?
My mama lavas me.

What do you get when you pour boiling water down a rabbit hole?
A hot cross bunny.

Riddlemaster answers:
Spoiled rabbit.
Hard-boiled eggs.
Boiled rabbit.

Why did the goofy guy laugh at the egg?
He thought it was a good yolk.

Riddlemaster answer:
It was cracking him up.

Why can't skeletons play music?
They have no organs.

Riddlemaster answers:
They already play trombones.
They got the groove.

Why was the computer injured?
It slipped a disk.

Riddlemaster answers:
The mouse ran into it.
It lost the motherboard.
It fell off his board surfing the Internet.
Somebody gave him a gigabyte.
It slipped on a web page.

How does a computer eat?
With megabytes.

Riddlemaster answer:
With microchips.

What do dancers drink when they're thirsty?
Tap water.

Riddlemaster answer:
Tang-O.

Why didn't the skeleton go to the dance?
It didn't have any body to take.

Riddlemaster answer:
It didn't have any guts.

HOOKED ON **RIDDLES**

How do cats do their shopping?
With a cat-alog.

Riddlemaster answer:
With a purrrrr-se.

What key cannot open a door?
A monkey.

Riddlemaster answer:
A map key.
A piano key.
Beef jer-key.

How can the alphabet change soup to make it taste bad?
Change it to soap.

Riddlemaster answer:
Make it sour.

Where is the best place for a haunted house?
On a dead end.

Riddlemaster answer:
On Blood Drive.

What's a ghost's favorite breakfast?
Dreaded wheat.

Riddlemaster answers:
Shredded sheet.
Booberry waffles.
Boo-Os.

Where do palm trees like to go?
On dates.

Riddlemaster answer:
Palm Springs.

What do monsters eat for breakfast?

How do you know when there's an elephant under your bed?
Your nose touches the ceiling.

Riddlemaster answer:
It's pretty stinky under there.

What do you get when you cross a vampire with a teacher?
A lot of blood tests.

Riddlemaster answer:
A bloodstitute.

Why did the cave talk so much?
Because it had a big mouth.

Riddlemaster answer:
It couldn't close its mouth.

What kind of candy makes you laugh?
Snickers.

Riddlemaster answer:
Laffy taffy.

What happens when bananas sunbathe?
They start to peel.

Riddlemaster answer:
They split.

How do cows count?
On a cow-culator.

Riddlemaster answer:
Mooo-tiplication.

The riddlemasters came up with the following gems by themselves! Check these out:

What did one fossil say to the other?
"Are you a fossil yet?"
"How old *are* you?"
"You look old!"

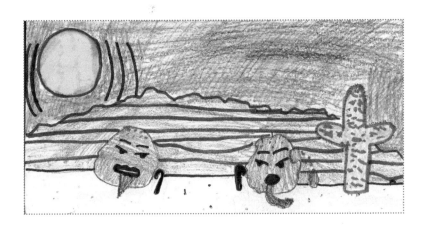

How is Mrs. Q like a tree?
Both have bark.

(Actually, if Mrs. Q had known who developed that riddle, that Riddlemaster would have probably spent another year in third grade!)

Chapter 8

The Magic of Riddles *or* Riddlemaster Originals!

We all strive to guide our little ones to that step where they can transfer what they're learning in the classroom and invent and create something original on their own, whether at school or at home. This happens after the students have comprehended, questioned, analyzed, and applied the concepts and material they've been taught.

It's a magic moment. It's a wondrous moment. It's the reward, besides the hugs, that teachers live for.

Once my riddlemasters had dug their creative minds into the marvelous world of riddles, they began the magic of inventing their own riddles. I'd like to share some examples of those spontaneous moments of riddle creativity in my classroom.

At Thanksgiving time we were preparing to decorate turkey cookies. I explained that after we decorated and ate the cookies, we were going to write about the experience, thus connecting this activity to a writing objective, that of writing a "how-to" composition.

Before we began, I read my students a composition that another third grader had written as an example. The selection was called: "How to Bathe a Mouse."

At the end of the reading, one of the riddlemasters added, "And that's how a mouse comes out squeaky clean. Hey, squeaky-clean! I could make that into a riddle! How does a mouse come out after a bath? Squeaky-clean! Hey, I just made up a riddle! Wow! Squeaky-clean! Get it? A mouse! Squeaky-clean!"

I just sat there and marveled as this chain of thought unfolded, the smile growing wider on his face as the ideas came out. He could barely contain himself!

Equally exciting was the time I told my third graders that they could write their own riddles and illustrate them after they had finished a test. I usually add a corresponding riddle or two as bonus questions at the end of tests but hadn't done that this time, so the Riddlemasters had liberty to write their own. As they finished up the test, they began the entertaining job of writing their own riddles for me.

I'll never forget watching one of my students who was usually reluctant to participate in class and who had become a true riddlemaster as she furiously scrawled riddle after riddle on her paper!

"Mrs. Q," she exclaimed, "I can't stop! These riddles keep popping into my head!"

That was a magic moment.

In the spring, my class develops our own riddle book in which the students have license to develop their own riddles, modify ones that they already know, or use a known riddle and illustrate it creatively. That is an opus to behold. It becomes our gift to ourselves, and gets printed up and sent out to our riddle suppliers during the year. There are all levels of concept acquisition from recall to synthesis in this delightful collection taken from these booklets.

Enjoy!

Here are some last recommendations for using riddles.

- Celebrate your riddlemasters' creativity. Give them ample opportunities to share riddles with you.
- Encourage them to create and illustrate their own riddles.
- Add riddles as a bonus question on a test or as a bonus question during any difficult activity. For example, Mrs. Q frequently has related science riddles as bonus questions on her science tests. Spelling tests sometimes have riddles that employ a spelling word or two.
- Help your youngsters make their own collections of riddles. You can use hand-drawn illustrations or let them delve into technology to develop their drawings.
- Remember, any question that requires you to play with words can be considered a riddle.
- Have fun! You are embarking on a wonderful adventure.

WHAT'S MINTY PASTY DANGEROUS AND KILLS GERMS?

SHARK-INFESTED TOOTHPASTE

What's white on the outside and green in the inside and hops?

A frog sandwich.

WHY CAN'T THE HOUSE JUMP HIGHER THAN THE MOUSE?

BECAUSE A HOUSE CAN'T JUMP!

What has a trunk and wheels but no engine?

An elephant on roller blades!

Why do teachers love springbreak?

Because they get vacation.

Why did the chicken cross the road, roll around in the dirt and cross the road again?

Because he wanted to be a dirty double crosser!

HOOKED ON **RIDDLES**

What do you get if a cow has only two legs?

Lean beef

Why do cows moo at the moon?

Mooo!

Because it is called the moon!

HOOKED ON RIDDLES

Why did the volcano erupt?

Because it was angry

Why didn't the bunny cross the road? Because it will get hit.	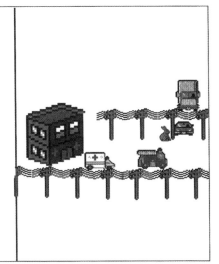

WHY DIDN'T THE
SKELETON CROSS THE
ROAD?

HE DIDN'T
HAVE THE
GUTS TO.

WHY DIDN'T THE SKELETON CROSS THE ROAD?

HE DIDN'T WANT TO BREAK HIS BONES.

Why do Moms like to shop?

They get free time from YOU!

Why was the computer sad when he drove home in his car?

He had a hard drive.

What kind of key won't work on a door?

A monkey!

Why did Mickey Mouse go to space?

To get Pluto!

Mrs. Quijano's Class
Riddles
Riddles
HeHeHe
Riddles
Spring 2001

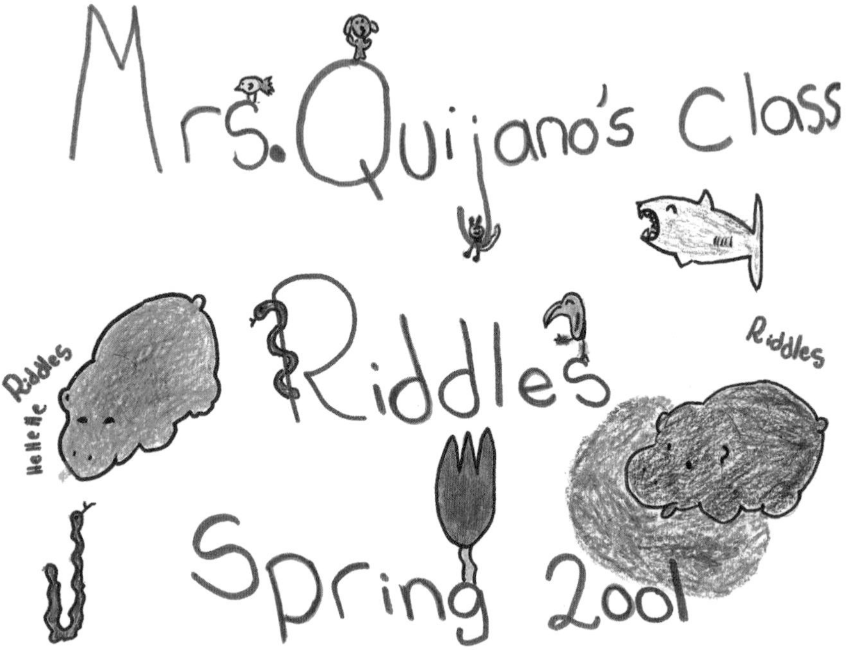

What did one fish say to the other fish?

Something smells fishy between us!!

Why did the ghost die in a Car wreck?

Because the seat belt went right through him.

Chapter 9

Adios *or* Apple-y Ever After

It's hard to say good-bye in most situations and especially at the end of the school year. After spending a whole year with my group of third graders, I have mixed feelings about the last day. Good-bye or *adios* means different things to each one. Next year there will be a few who occasionally come by to say hello on their way to their fourth-grade classroom. Some have even come back once they're in high school and have stood outside my classroom waiting for me to recognize them. Their greeting is always the same: "You don't remember me, do you?" Silly question!

So how do you make an impression that will last? I ask former students to share their favorite memories of third grade with me. The formula for lasting memories seems to involve two important factors: anything that strays from the norm and any unique activity that becomes part of the routine in the classroom. One activity that most students recall with a smile is the construction of the baking soda and vinegar volcano. It's one time when we do something that's not usually allowed in the classroom . . . make a stinky mess. I let them twist my arm into using more baking soda and vinegar than is necessary, thus creating a flow of *lava* that runs over everything and leaves the room smelling like vinegar longer than I'd prefer.

Routinely injecting riddles into your interaction with children provides that unique activity that they can rely on and remember for years. Adding an anonymous supplier of riddles enhances the delight as it affords a mysterious component along with the guarantee that there will always be riddles.

At least weekly, in the halls, in the cafeteria, at dismissal time, or as a former student comes in to say "hello," I will get the same question from past riddlemasters: "Has Mr. Riddle sent any mas lately?"

Your outside riddle source doesn't have to be a Mr. Riddle, although you'd be surprised how many people out there enjoy sharing riddles. Your source can be a riddle book or an Internet site. Riddle books can be found in ample supply in bookstores, libraries, and even on kids' book orders from school! Each morning on my way to school, the radio station intersperses its music with kid-friendly riddles. While waiting my turn at the dentist the other day, I noticed a stack of kids' books on the table next to the magazines. Right under a cute beginner book about teeth was—you guessed it—a beginner book of riddles! They're everywhere!

This book alone has enough riddles to last you an entire year.

Now that you know that there is a seemingly endless supply of riddles out there, it's up to you to start enjoying! You're guaranteed to find your own ways to use riddles to your delight and the delight of your riddlemasters. And for those times when you don't have any riddles handy, chances are very good that your riddlemasters will have some to share with you. You will find that as you use riddles, you too become addicted to the pleasure of figuring out the answers.

Kids are born *riddle-ready*. It's up to you to help them become *riddle-reactive*. They'll love you for it. They'll appreciate the chance to squeal in delight as you bend the rules a bit and add more baking soda to the volcano of life!

I treasure the opportunity to work with kids. Working with and being around kids keeps my spirit young. My own kids are all grown up but they still enjoy hearing the stories I bring home from school and they've gotten accustomed to being treated to unexpected riddles. I now have a young grandson whose favorite activity in the car is sharing riddles. What a delight!

I appreciate the friends who have shared riddles with our class. Special thanks go to our dedicated and creative friend, Mr. Riddle, far away in Riddle Command. Mr. Riddle's constant supply of mas has helped create a learning experience that is always fun, challenging, and full of surprises. As time went on, he became more specific with the riddles or "mas" that were sent our way. Friday was always monster mas day. Other days of the week reflected a theme, usually with a title rich in alliteration.

Mas would have a title in the subject line to idenify the theme of the riddles. I would sometimes read the subject line and ask my third graders what they thought the riddles would be about.

Eventually I started asking for a riddle they thought would be found in that group of mas. We went from main idea to supporting details!

This chapter of riddles has a collection of subject lines with an accompanying riddle for each title.

I also want to thank you for caring enough about the kids in your life, whether they're your own, or ones you work with daily in school, day care, or just the neighborhood kids who seem to wander into your heart and home. I encourage you to try out riddles as a daily supplement. Soon you will find that you need darker sunglasses because your riddlemasters are so bright!

Finally, and most importantly, a big thanks to the riddlemasters who bless my life. Because of them, every school year ends the same way the story about the apple ends.

That would be: Apple-y ever after.

RIDDLES: Subject Lines for Daily Mas

Mondays

Wake up Monday Mas
Why do we go to bed?
Because the bed can't come to us.

Mane-ly Monday Mas
How do lions like their meat cooked?
Medium roar.

Top-o-the Morning Monday Mas (March 17)
What's long and green and has thousands of feet?
A St. Patrick's Day Parade.

Moo-nday Moo Mas
What do you call a place full of ancient cows?
A mooseum.

Mish Mosh Monday Mas
Where do you go to replace a missing chess piece?
To the pawnshop.

Money Monday Moolah Mas
What do you call rich air?
Millionaire.

HOOKED on **RIDDLES**

Meanie Monday Mas

When was the cook mean?

When he beat the eggs.

Military Monday Mas
Who are the youngest members of the army?
The infantry.

Just a Minute Monday Mas
Why did the goofy kid sit on her watch?
She wanted to be on time.

Everything Ducky Monday Mas
What did the chicken say to the duck?
"You quack me up!"

Mallard Monday Mas
What time do ducks wake up in the morning?
At the quack of dawn.

Musical Monday Mas
How did the new music teacher brush his teeth?
With a tuba toothpaste.

Monkey Monday Mas
What kind of ice cream do monkeys eat?
Chocolate chimp.

Marine Monday Mas
What does a whale do when it's sad?
Blubber.

Meteorological Monday Mas
Why don't weather forecasters tell each other jokes?
They don't want to laugh up a storm.

Meow Mix Monday Mas
What do cats drive?
Catillacs.

Mardi Monday Fat City Shrove Mas
How did the kid feel after eating 100 pancakes?
He felt waffle.

Meaty Monday Mas
Is there a way to make a hamburger do the hula?
Order it with a shake.

Motoring Monday Mas
What do baby cars wear in the rain?
Windshield diapers.

Super Monday Mas
Why did the football player hit the vending machine?
To get his quarterback.

Tuesdays

Tasty Toozday Mas
Why did the boy bring peanut butter to the beach?
Because he heard there were jellyfish.

Toasty Tuesday Mas
What does a slice of toast wear to bed?
Jammies.

Trimming Tuesday Mas
What did the conductor say to the barber?
"Take it from the top!"

Looking Good Taking Care Tuesday Mas
Why did the woman put makeup on her forehead?
So she could make up her mind.

Hop-to-Toozday Mas
What kind of shoes do frogs wear?
Open toad.

Title 'em Tuesday Mas
What do you call a chicken who thinks he's Superman?
Cluck Kent.

Too Too Easy Toozday Mas
What has four wheels and flies?
A garbage truck.

Terrarium Tuesday Roots Mas
What happened to the flowers who misbehaved for Mother Earth?
They were grounded.

Two-fer Twosday Mas
What do you get when you cross a cow and a duck?
Milk and quackers.

Turtle Tuesday Mas
What do well-dressed turtles wear?
People-neck sweaters.

Tricky Talky Tuesday Mas
What is the opposite of ice cream?
You whisper.

Twisty Tricky Tuesday Mas
What is the best way to go down a slide?
Slideways.

Take-off Tuesday Space Mas

How does an astronaut put a baby to sleep?
Rock-et.

Chicken on Tuesday Mas
Why do chickens go to museums?
To see the eggshibits.

Tweet Tweet Tuesday Bird Mas
What bird is with you at every meal?
A swallow.

Later Gator Tuesday Mas
What do you get if you cross an alligator with a pickle?
A croco-dill.

Transportation Tuesday Mas
What do you call an insect's car?
A buggy.

Treetop Tuesday Mas
What did the rake say to the tree?
Don't leave.

HOOKED ON **RIDDLES**

Compu-Toozday Mas
How can you tell when a cat was at the computer?
The mouse is missing.

Massive Monday and Tusks on Tuesday Mas (After a Monday holiday)
Why are elephants so wrinkled?
They're hard to iron.

Wednesdays

Ask Why Wednesday Mas
Why would Snow White make a good judge?
Because she was the fairest in all the land.

What's It Wednesday Mas
What is always coming but never arrives?
Tomorrow. When it arrives, it's today.

Where Is It Wednesday States of the Union Geography Mas
What state can you wear?
New Jersey.

What's the Difference Wednesday Mas
What's the difference between a flea and a dog?
A dog can have fleas, but a flea can't have dogs.

When-is Wednesday Mas
When is a door not a door?
When it's ajar.

Whatcha Call It Wednesday Mas
What do you call a flying turtle?
A shellicopter.

Who's It Wednesday Mas
Why did the soldier salute his refrigerator?
Because it was General Electric.

What to Eat Wednesday Mas
What does a camera like to eat?
Cheese.

Way Out Wednesday Mas
Why did the moon stop eating?
Because it was full.

Name Game Wednesday Mas
What did the iguana keeper name her daughter?
Liz

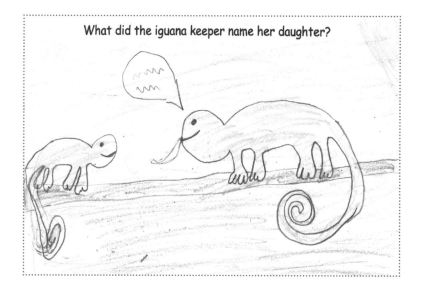

Whale of a Wednesday Mas
What do whales like to chew?
Blubber gum.

Workin' Wednesday Mas
Where do people who work at ice cream stands get educated?
In sundae school.

Walkin' Wednesday Mas
Why did the yardstick have trouble buying shoes?
Because it had three feet.

Wicked Weather Wednesday Mas
What do clouds wear under their raincoats?
Thunderwear.

What's Up Wednesday Mas
What gets heavier when you use it?
A towel.

What Do They Say Wednesday Mas
What did the rug say to the floor?
"I've got you covered!"

Bow-wow Wednesday Mas
Why did the police officer give the dog a ticket?
For double barking.

Time after Time Wednesday Mas
What has a face but no mouth?
A clock.

Wiggly Wednesday Mas
What do snakes put on their kitchen floors?
Reptiles.

Winging Wednesday Mas
Why do seagulls live near the sea instead of the bay?
Because if they lived near the bay, they would be called bagels.

Plumb Crazy Now It's Wednesday Mas
What do you call a plumber's new assistant?
A drainee.

Thursdays

Think about It Thursday Mas
If a plane traveling from Canada to California crashes in Montana, where do they bury the survivors?
They don't bury survivors.

There It Is Thursday Mas
If the Red House is on the right and the Blue House is on the left, then where is the White House?
In Washington, D.C.

Up in the Air Thursday Mas
What do fireflies eat?
Light snacks.

Thloppy Thursday Mas
What do you get if you don't clean your mirror?
A dirty look.

In Your Face Thursday Mas
What thing do you always overlook?
Your nose.

Thirsty Thursday Mas
What's a boxer's favorite drink?
Punch.

Thilly Thcratchy Thursday Mas
Why did the clock scratch?
Because it had ticks.

Singing Thursday Mas
How do fish practice singing?
They use scales.

Slippery Thursday Mas
What do you call two bananas?
A pair of slippers.

Tight Thtuff Thursday Mas

What do you get when you have 324 blueberries trying to get through the same door?

A blueberry jam.

Talk to the Animals Thursday Mas

Why can't you have a conversation with a ram?

Because it keeps butting in.

Trunk Packin' Thursday Mas
What is blue and gray and huge?
An elephant holding its breath.

Totally Bananas Thursday Mas Bunch
What's yellow and writes?
A ballpoint banana.

Roostin' Thursday Mas
Why can't a rooster ever get rich?
Because he works for chicken feed.

Never Sick of Thursday Mas
What does a doctor give a sick bird?
Tweetment.

Clothes Call Thursday Mas
Why did the golfer wear two pairs of pants?
In case he got a hole in one.

Thinking Thursday School Mas
What's smarter than a talking parrot?
A spelling bee.

Think Hard Thursday Mas
Super challenge for the Riddlemasters: What does this say?
(Write it on the board.)
YY U R YY I C U R YY 4 ME.
Answer: "Too Wise, you are too wise. I see you are too wise for me!"

Muy Mas Monster Mas
What did the monsters have for dinner last night?
Ghoulash.

Fridays

Friday Monster Mas
What do witches put on their hair?
Scare spray.

HOOKED ON **RIDDLES**

Last day of school

Marching Out Monday Last Tag Ain't No Mas
What did the third grade teacher say when the year ended?
"Go forth!"

Chapter 10

Rhyme Time *or* Hink Pinks Just for You

O h it's rhyming time, my friend, I'm gonna leave you . . .
As a parting gift, I'd like to offer you some fairly easy riddles to try your hand at answering. These are called hink pinks, which are fun riddles that have a pair of rhyming words as their answer. They're great for lessons filled with rhyming words and synonyms. The answer is always composed of two rhyming words.

For example:

What's a nice number?
Fine nine.

HOOKED ON **RIDDLES**

I've mentioned many times throughout this book how important it is to give your riddlemasters clues when trying to decipher riddles. So for you, dear reader, I have two clues to aid you in answering each hink pink. One clue will be given in the picture that our Riddlemaster has drawn, and the other clue is the fact that each answer is made up of two rhyming words. Easy, right? You decide. At any rate, you may look at the end of the chapter for the answer if you are completely stumped, but I bet you won't be like that mountain and peek!

You're on the way to your own riddle adventure. Enjoy these hink pinks, just for you!

Before you begin, these are your reminders:

- Hink pinks have two rhyming words in the answer.

- Think of synonyms to the words in the question, and you'll come up with the answer.

- Have fun!

RIDDLES: Hink Pinks Just for You

What do you call an angry father?

What's a huge truck?

huge

small

What is a nice law?

What's a seafood spread?

What's a spicy place?

What do you call a Chubby kitty?

What is a cute young cat?

What's a naked rabbit?

What is a fancy barn?

HOOKED ON **RIDDLES**

whats a fat sandwich.

What's a cooked reptile?

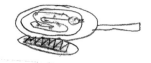

What's a meat burglar?

What does a girl take to smell pretty?

Check your answers!

1. *What do you call an angry father?*
Answer: A mad dad.

2. *What's a huge truck?*
Answer: A big rig.

3. *What is a nice law?*
Answer: A cool rule.

4. *What's a seafood spread?*
Answer: Clam jam.

5. *What's a spicy place?*
Answer: A hot spot.

6. *What do you call a chubby kitty?*
Answer: A fat cat.

7. *What is a cute young cat?*
Answer: A pretty kitty.

8. *What's a naked rabbit?*
Answer: A bare hare.

9. *What is a fancy barn?*
Answer: Charm farm.

10. *What's a fat sandwich?*
Answer: A chub sub.

11. *What's a cooked reptile?*
Answer: Baked snake.

HOOKED ON **RIDDLES**

12. What's a meat burglar?

Answer: A beef thief

13. What does a girl take to smell pretty?

Answer: A flower shower.

Acknowledgments and thanks go to the following people:

HOOKED ON **RIDDLES**

To my family for your support and for never tiring of my silly stories and riddles.

To Mr. Riddle for being my faithful riddle supplier.

HOOKED ON **RIDDLES**

To my friends Tom Feran and Mark Dawidziak, both reporters at the *Cleveland Plain Dealer* for your insight and encouragement. Tom's two columns in the *Plain Dealer* documenting my classroom riddle adventure years ago provided the magic that launched and fueled this project. I couldn't have done it without you!

To my third graders at Longs Creek Elementary. Without you this book would not have its riddlicious illustrations. You provided them all!

HOOKED ON **RIDDLES**

About the Author

Mary Quijano grew up in Cleveland, Ohio. After college she went to Honduras as a Peace Corps Volunteer and lived there for twelve years, teaching at a bilingual school after her service ended. You can read about some of her Honduran adventures in a book called *Gather the Fruit One by One*, a collection of amazing Peace Corps Stories written by former volunteers in the Americas. She currently teaches third grade at Longs Creek Elementary in the North East Independent School District in San Antonio, Texas, where she continues to enjoy the riddle adventure with her students. When she's not teaching, Mary loves to travel and explore new places. She lives with her husband and family in San Antonio, Texas.

Make Your Own Riddles!

Please use the following pages to make up your own riddles
and the illustrations to match. Have fun!